Fly Like the Eagle

By Jay Sanders
Illustrated by Nick Bland

Chapter 1 *Good as Gold* 2

Chapter 2 *Where Is Mrs Canon?* 6

Chapter 3 *A Special Surprise* 10

Chapter 1

Good as Gold

"Hello, Mrs Canon," said Riley as he pushed open the big glass doors. "How are you today?"

"As good as gold, Riley," smiled Mrs Canon, the librarian, "as good as gold."

Every Friday after school, Riley and his Grandad went to the town library. Riley always went straight to the children's book section and chose four picture story books to take home. Grandad always sat in a big chair and read the newspaper.

Mrs Canon had worked at the library for as long as Riley could remember. Sometimes, if she wasn't too busy at the desk, she would read Riley a story.

They both had lots of favourites ... *The Giving Tree*, *Grandma Chicken Legs* and *Peter and the Wolf*. But the story Riley loved to hear time and time again was an old African story called *Fly, Eagle, Fly!*

The story was about an eagle that thought it was a chicken. Until one day it learned it was much more than that, and could fly high above the mountains.

Mrs Canon would often say, "One day you will fly like the eagle and read this story to me!"

Fly, Eagle, Fly!

Chapter 2

Where Is Mrs Canon?

The following Friday, Riley and Grandad went to the library as usual. When they went through the big glass doors they were both surprised to see that Mrs Canon was not behind the desk.

In her place was a tall man with round glasses.

"Hello," said Riley, "where is Mrs Canon today?"

"I'm very sorry to say," replied the tall man, "Mrs Canon had an accident last Tuesday and had to be taken to hospital. She slipped over on her way to the bus stop. I'm afraid she has broken her leg in two places."

Riley's face fell. "Poor Mrs Canon," he said.

"How long will she be in hospital?" asked Grandad.

"She'll be there for about a week," answered the man, "and then she has to rest at home for another three weeks."

"Oh, dear me!" said Grandad.

H~
O
P~

Chapter 3

A Special Surprise

When Riley and Grandad got home, they told Gran about Mrs Canon.

"Oh no!" said Gran. "Poor Mrs Canon."

"Can we go and visit her at the hospital tomorrow?" asked Riley.

"Yes," answered Gran. "That's a good idea."

"We could make her a cake," said Riley.

"Yes," smiled Gran, "that's an even better idea!"

"And," said Grandad smiling at Riley, "we've got another very special surprise for Mrs Canon, haven't we Riley?"

"Yes," said Riley with a big grin.

On Saturday morning Riley and Gran baked a cake for Mrs Canon. Grandad picked some of his best pink roses from the garden, and then they all took the bus to the hospital.

“Hello, Mrs Canon,” said Riley as he peeped around the hospital door. “How are you today?”

“As good as gold,” replied Mrs Canon with a brave smile. “As good as gold.”

Riley, Gran and Grandad sat on some chairs near Mrs Canon's bed.

"Gran and I made you a cake," said Riley, "and Grandad picked you some roses from his garden."

"Thank you all very much," said Mrs Canon. A little tear ran down her pale cheek.

"It is so kind of you to visit me."

Riley smiled at Mrs Canon. "I have another surprise for you," he said.

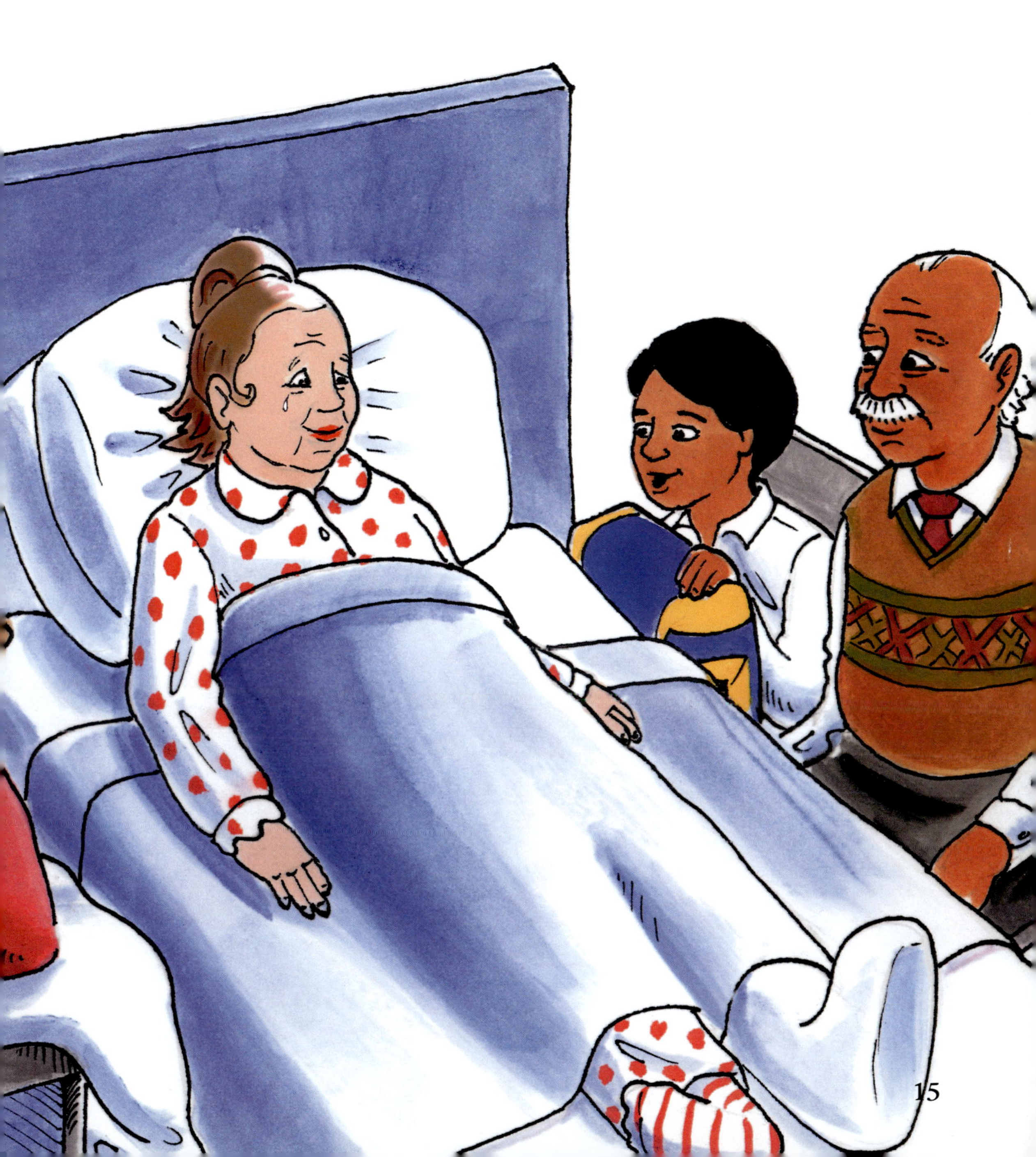

Riley took *Fly, Eagle, Fly!* out of his back pack and began to read.

He read each word very carefully, just as he had practised the night before with Grandad.

When the last sentence was finished, he looked up at Mrs Canon and smiled.

"Riley," she said returning his smile, "I'm very proud of you. I always knew one day you would fly like the eagle!"